101 THINGS TO CHEER UP A GRUMPY OLD GIT

First published in 2023 by Allsorted Ltd WD19 4BG U.K.

ISBN 9781915902184

Printed in Croatia.

101 THINGS TO
CHEER UP A
GRUMPY OLD GIT

INTRODUCTION

Life can sometimes seem like a never-ending list of irritations, leaving us feeling grumpy and out of sorts. '**101 Things to Cheer Up a Grumpy Old Git**' is the perfect antidote to those irksome moments. Packed with light-hearted trivia, humorous quotes, and laugh-out-loud anecdotes, it offers a delightful distraction from the everyday gripes. Whether you're the grumpy git, or you're looking to lift the spirits of someone who is, this book serves up a delightful assortment of cheerfulness. Dive in and rediscover the lighter side of life with this amusing and entertaining collection.

"MIDDLE AGE IS WHEN
YOUR AGE STARTS TO
SHOW AROUND
YOUR MIDDLE."

BOB HOPE

FUNNY FORGOTTEN WORDS

Gadzooks: An exclamation of surprise or annoyance, popular in the seventeenth and eighteenth centuries.

Lollygag: To spend time aimlessly or to dawdle; its usage peaked in the nineteenth and early twentieth centuries.

Flapdoodle: Nonsense or foolish talk used in the nineteenth century.

Flibbertigibbet: A frivolous or flighty person; the word was popular in the fifteenth to nineteenth centuries.

Bumbershoot: A colloquial term for an umbrella, (derived from the US) used primarily in the late nineteenth and early twentieth centuries.

Hornswoggle: To deceive or cheat someone; this term was popular in the nineteenth century.

Snollygoster: A shrewd, unprincipled person, especially a politician; used in the nineteenth and early twentieth centuries.

OLDEST RECORDED PERSON

Born in the sunny South of France in 1875, **Jeanne Calment** experienced two World Wars and was an eyewitness to significant global change. Remarkably, she lived independently until the age of 110. She had an extraordinarily long life, reaching the unparalleled age of 122.

WAITING AT TRAFFIC LIGHTS

A UK study suggested the average motorist spends approximately **48 hours every year** waiting at traffic lights. This translates to two full days. That's a lot of nose picking, snacking and goodness knows what else.

108 YEARS OLD AND STILL WORKING

At the age of 96, US-Italian barber **Mancinelli** entered Guinness World Records as the world's oldest practising barber. He started working as a barber when he was just 12, dropped out of high school to work full time and overcame a lung infection caused by inhaling hair clippings at the age of 27. Mancinelli died in 2019 at the age of 108 after reluctantly retiring from work only a few weeks before.

"THERE IS ONLY ONE
CURE FOR GREY HAIR.
IT WAS INVENTED BY
A FRENCHMAN. IT IS
CALLED THE GUILLOTINE."

P. G. WODEHOUSE

SILLY ANIMAL GROUP NAMES

A parliament of owls

A crash of rhinoceroses

A murder of crows

A business of ferrets

A tower of giraffes

A knot of toads

A romp of otters

A prickle of porcupines

A flamboyance of flamingos

A clowder of cats

"A PESSIMIST IS A PERSON WHO HAS HAD TO LISTEN TO TOO MANY OPTIMISTS."

DON MARQUIS

"THE SECRET OF STAYING YOUNG IS TO LIVE HONESTLY, EAT SLOWLY, AND LIE ABOUT YOUR AGE."

LUCILLE BALL

TIME WASTERS

Research indicates that individuals in Britain lose up to **26 days** per year due to inefficiencies, including lengthy waits on phone calls, channel surfing on television, and even waiting for the kettle to boil to make a cup of tea.

CUBE-SHAPED POOP

Wombats, unique Australian marsupials, produce cube-shaped poop! This distinct shape, a result of their digestive process, prevents the droppings from rolling away, enabling wombats to effectively mark their territory with these oddly-shaped calling cards.

TYPICAL VIKING INSULTS

'You have the strength of a starving goat!'

'You're as brave as a sheep!'

'Your sword is as dull as your wits!'

'You're as slow as a glacier!'

'You have the heart of a troll!'

'You're as fierce as a wet cat!'

'You're as useful as a wooden sword!'

"A CYNIC IS A MAN WHO,
WHEN HE SMELLS
FLOWERS, LOOKS
AROUND FOR A COFFIN."

H. L. MENCKEN

LIST OF STRANGE PHOBIAS

Ablutophobia: Fear of washing or cleaning oneself.

Arachibutyrophobia: Fear of peanut butter sticking to the roof of one's mouth.

Barophobia: Fear of gravity or the sensation of being crushed by gravity.

Chionophobia: Fear of snow or snowy weather.

Dendrophobia: Fear of trees or wooded areas.

Euphobia: Fear of hearing good news.

Genuphobia: Fear of knees or the act of kneeling.

Heliophobia: Fear of sunlight or bright light.

Ichthyophobia: Fear of fish, whether alive or dead.

Koumpounophobia: Fear of buttons on clothing.

Lachanophobia: Fear of vegetables.

Mageirocophobia: Fear of cooking or being in a kitchen.

Nomophobia: Fear of being without a mobile phone or losing mobile signal.

Ombrophobia: Fear of rain or being rained on.

Pogonophobia: Fear of beards or people with beards.

Scriptophobia: Fear of writing in public or being judged for one's writing.

Triskaidekaphobia: Fear of the number 13.

Urophobia: Fear of urine or urination.

Venustraphobia: Fear of beautiful women.

Xylophobia: Fear of wooden objects or forests.

INTERESTING STORIES ABOUT COMEDIANS

Before he became famous, **Jim Carrey** wrote himself a cheque for $10 million for 'acting services rendered' and dated it for five years in the future. He kept the cheque in his wallet, and by the time the date arrived, he had achieved significant success in his acting career and had the money to cash the cheque.

Whoopi Goldberg worked as a mortuary beautician and a bricklayer before finding success as a comedian and actress.

"I WISH MORE PEOPLE
WERE FLUENT IN SILENCE."

ANONYMOUS

AMUSING ANIMAL NAMES

Dik-Dik: A small species of antelope in the Genus Madoqua that lives in the bushlands of eastern and southern Africa.

Aye-Aye: A type of lemur found in Madagascar with a unique method of finding food called 'percussive foraging'.

Tasselled Wobbegong: A species of carpet shark found in the shallow coral reefs off northern Australia, and around New Guinea.

Fangtooth Fish: A beryciform fish found in the deep waters of many of the world's oceans.

Pink Fairy Armadillo: The smallest species of armadillo, native to central Argentina.

Proboscis Monkey: A monkey known for its large nose, found on the island of Borneo in southeast Asia.

Leafy Seadragon: A marine fish related to the seahorse, found along the southern and western coasts of Australia.

Blue-Footed Booby: A marine bird native to subtropical and tropical regions of the Pacific Ocean, known for its distinctive bright blue feet.

Kakapo: A flightless, nocturnal parrot native to New Zealand.

Wunderpus Photogenicus: A species of octopus found in the waters of Indonesia and Malaysia.

"ANYBODY WHO TOLD
YOU TO BE YOURSELF
SIMPLY COULDN'T
HAVE GIVEN YOU
WORSE ADVICE."

RUSSELL LYNES

AN UNFORTUNATE CONFESSION

In 2009, a man named **James Washington** suffered a heart attack while in police custody in Nashville, Tennessee. Believing he was about to die, he confessed to a 17-year-old unsolved murder.

However, he survived the heart attack and tried to recant his confession. His 'alibi' was that he'd only confessed to get medical attention for his heart attack, hoping to avoid death.
He was convicted of the murder.

NAMES OF TOWNS AND VILLAGES

Accident (Maryland, USA)

Bald Knob (Arkansas, USA)

Boring (Oregon, USA)

Catbrain (England)

Climax (Georgia, USA)

Ding Dong (Texas, USA)

Hell (Michigan USA)

Middelfart (Denmark)

No Place (England)

Punkeydoodles Corners (Ontario, Canada)

Saint-Louis-du-Ha! Ha! (Quebec, Canada)

Scratchy Bottom (England)

Shitterton (England)

Toad Suck (Arkansas, USA)

THE WORLD'S LONGEST SNEEZING FIT

The longest sneezing fit on record is attributed to **Donna Griffiths** from Worcestershire, England. She began sneezing on 13 January 1981, and continued to sneeze for an astounding 976 days, with the sneezing fit finally ending on 16 September 1983. This unique case has earned her a place in the Guinness World Records.

"I DON'T BELIEVE IN ASTROLOGY; I'M A SAGITTARIUS AND WE'RE SCEPTICAL."

ARTHUR C. CLARKE

BIZARRE FOODS FROM AROUND THE WORLD

Hákarl: Fermented shark (Iceland)

Balut: Duck embryo (Philippines)

Casu Marzu: Cheese with live maggots (Sardinia)

Century Eggs: (China)

Haggis: Sheep's stomach (Scotland)

Surströmming: Fermented herring (Sweden)

Rocky Mountain Oysters: Bulls' testicles (USA)

Witchetty Grub: (Australia)

Mopane Worms: (Zimbabwe)

Durian: Fruit known for its strong odour (southeast Asia)

LEGENDARY SILLY DEATHS

Aeschylus (c.525/524 – 456/455 BC):
This ancient Greek tragedian died when an eagle,
mistaking his bald head for a rock, dropped a
tortoise on him in an attempt to crack its shell.

Draco (c. Seventh-century BC):
The Athenian lawmaker died from suffocation
when his supporters, in an attempt to show their
approval, threw so many hats and cloaks on him
that he was unable to breathe.

Hans Steininger (1567):
Hans Steininger – the burgomaster of the town
of Braunau am Inn, Austria – was known for
his exceptionally long beard. He died when he
tripped over his beard while trying
to escape a fire.

MOSQUITOES AND BANANAS

According to some studies, **mosquitoes** are more attracted to people who have recently eaten bananas. The exact reasons for this are not clear, but it's suggested that certain chemicals in bananas could be the cause.

BEST THING SINCE SLICED BREAD

Otto Frederick Rohwedder, an American inventor, created the first automatic bread-slicing machine for bakeries in 1928. This innovation revolutionized the baking industry and led to the popular phrase 'the best thing since sliced bread'.

THE DISHWASHER

The dishwasher was invented by **Josephine Cochrane**, an American socialite who was tired of her servants chipping her fine china while washing the dishes. In 1886, she patented her design: the first commercially successful dishwashing machine.

ASTRONAUTS' BURPING CONUNDRUM

Due to the lack of gravity in space, **astronauts** cannot burp. The lack of gravity prevents the separation of gas and liquids in their stomachs, making it impossible to burp normally.

RECORD-BREAKING GOLDFISH

Tish, the world's oldest goldfish, lived for 43 years in the UK. Won at a fair in 1956, his longevity was due to his owners' diligent care. His colour faded in old age, and he passed away in 1999.

LIFE AFTER DEATH

In 1945, an American farmer decapitated a chicken, named **Mike**, intending to eat him. However, Mike survived. Fed with an eyedropper, Mike lived headless for 18 months.

CORPORATE PRANKS

Google (2007) – Google TiSP: Google announced a free in-home wireless broadband service called 'TiSP', which purportedly worked through your toilet and sewage systems.

Burger King (1998) – Left-Handed Whopper: Burger King ran an advertisement in USA Today announcing a new 'Left-Handed Whopper' specifically designed for left-handed burger lovers.

Virgin Atlantic (2018) – Flights to Mars: Richard Branson and Virgin Atlantic claimed they would be launching the first commercial flight to Mars.

IKEA (2017) – Barkingham Palace Dog House:
IKEA Australia announced a high-tech dog house, complete with an air purifier, a doggy spa, and an automatic food dispenser.

BBC (1957) – Swiss Spaghetti Harvest:
The BBC broadcast a report on the Swiss spaghetti harvest, showing women carefully plucking strands of spaghetti from a tree and laying them in the sun to dry.

Amazon (2020) – Introducing Amazon Dating:
This prank was a play on Amazon's website, advertising a dating service where you could 'buy' a date.

"THE WORLD IS FULL OF PEOPLE LOOKING FOR SPECTACULAR HAPPINESS WHILE THEY SNUB CONTENTMENT."

DOUG LARSON

COMPLETELY BANANAS

Believe it or not, we're about 50% identical to **bananas** at the DNA level! This doesn't make us half fruit, but it does show we share many life building blocks. The rest of our DNA? That's what makes us uniquely human and bananas decidedly, well, bananas!

ASTRONAUTS' HEIGHT IN SPACE

In the zero-gravity conditions of space, **astronauts** experience a slight increase in height, sometimes up to 2 inches. This happens as the spine stretches out without Earth's gravity. But this is temporary—once they return to Earth and its gravity, they go back to their original height.

"ALWAYS FORGIVE YOUR ENEMIES; NOTHING ANNOYS THEM SO MUCH."

OSCAR WILDE

WHY DID THE CHICKEN CROSS THE ROAD?

IT DIDN'T, IT BECAME ROADKILL.

OPERATION ACOUSTIC KITTY

In a project called '**Acoustic Kitty**', the CIA attempted to use cats as spies during the Cold War. The plan was to implant microphones in cats and release them near Soviet compounds. Despite the intrigue, the plan wasn't successful and was quickly shelved. Even for spies, cats are hard to train!

"TO ME, OLD AGE IS ALWAYS 15 YEARS OLDER THAN I AM."

BERNARD BARUCH

LIST OF ONOMATOPOEIAS

Murmur	Swoosh	Crunch
Fizz	Flutter	Slap
Rustle	Hiccup	Whack
Jingle	Plop	Grumble
Slam	Drip	Munch
Gush	Squelch	Clatter
Whirl	Thump	

LAUGHTER STATS

On average, an adult **laughs** about 17 times a day. Laughter, apart from being a response to humour, also serves as a way of communicating, bonding, and even as a form of therapy.

TIM PPPPPPPPPRICE

A British man changed his name by deed poll to **Tim Pppppppppprice** to make it harder for telemarketers to pronounce. He refers to himself as Tim '10p' Price.

WHAT KIND OF TEA IS HARD TO SWALLOW?

REALITY.

HOLLOW EARTH THEORY

The **Hollow Earth theory** is an old concept suggesting our planet is entirely hollow or contains substantial interior space. Some believe mythical creatures or ancient civilizations reside within. Although captivating, it's scientifically unsupported by all those except supporters of hollow head theory.

EMPEROR CLAUDIUS AND DINING ETIQUETTE

Emperor Claudius, who reigned from AD 41 to AD 54, was said to have considered a decree allowing people to expel gas at the dining table to promote better health, after hearing of someone who nearly died trying to hold it in.

"I USED TO HAVE A HANDLE ON LIFE, BUT THEN IT BROKE."

ANONYMOUS

UNIQUE NAME CHANGE

In 2007, an Australian man named **Chris Sands** legally changed his name to 'Captain Fantastic Faster Than Superman Spiderman Batman Wolverine Hulk And The Flash Combined'.

BARCODES

The first product to be scanned with a barcode in a shop was a pack of **Wrigley'**s chewing gum in 1974, in Ohio.

PING-PONG BALLS

Ping-pong balls are so light that they can float on air currents, which is why players sometimes blow on the ball to clean it rather than pick it up.

GOLF BALLS

Modern **golf balls** have between 300–500 dimples.

PIRATE VS GOVERNOR BOUNTY

Faced with a $500 bounty on his head, infamous pirate **Jean Lafitte** turned the tables on the governor who had issued it: Lafitte issued his own bounty on the governor's head – for $5000! Unfortunately for Lafitte the bounty hunters never did manage to hunt down the governor.

CHICKEN POPULATION

There are more than 25 billion **chickens** worldwide, more than four times the human population.

HAPPINESS IN OLDER ADULTS

Research suggests that **older adults** have better emotional regulation skills and are generally happier compared to younger adults.

ICEBERG AIRCRAFT CARRIER

During the **Second World War**, the British government developed a plan to turn an iceberg into an aircraft carrier. However, the plan was ultimately scrapped due to technical difficulties and the risk of the iceberg capsizing.

"THE BEST WAY TO REMEMBER YOUR WIFE'S BIRTHDAY IS TO FORGET IT ONCE."

H. V. PROCHNOW

THE LOUDEST RECORDED BURP

Neville 'Foghorn' Sharp from Australia holds the Guinness Word Record for the loudest burp. He set this record on 4 February 2020 with a burp that measured 112.4 decibels.
This is louder than a trombone.

PET ROCK PHENOMENON

In the 1970s, a man named **Gary Dahl** packaged and sold ordinary rocks as pets, complete with care instructions and a 'Pet Rock Training Manual'. Despite its simplicity, the Pet Rock became a fad and sold millions of units as a humorous novelty item.

TOILET TIME VS EXERCISE TIME

The average adult spends more time on the **toilet** than they do exercising. In fact, over an entire lifetime studies suggest the average person spends over 1.5 years on the toilet.

LARGEST SHOE SIZE IN HISTORY

The largest shoe size ever recorded belongs to **Robert Wadlow**, who is recognised as the tallest person in recorded history. Wadlow's shoe size was a staggering 37AA (US size), equivalent to approximately 75 (Europe), or 36 (UK). His feet were 47cm or 18.5 inches long.

OLDEST JOKES EVER RECORDED

Ancient Greece – AD 300–400:
A pedant tried to teach his donkey not to eat by withholding food. When the donkey died of hunger, he lamented, 'I've had a great loss! Just when he had learned not to eat, he died.'

Ancient Rome – 63 BC to AD 14:
Emperor Augustus noticed a man in the crowd who looked like him and asked if his mother had worked at the palace. The man replied, 'No, your highness, but my father did.'

DON'T YOU HATE IT WHEN SOMEONE ANSWERS THEIR OWN QUESTIONS?

I DO.

THE GREAT EMU WAR

The "**Great Emu War**" of 1932 was a government-sanctioned military operation in Australia, targeting emus that damaged crops in Western Australia. Unexpectedly resilient, the emus evaded the soldiers' attempts at control, leading to the operation's eventual withdrawal after a month of comedic failures.

THE DANCING PLAGUE OF 1518

In **Strasbourg**, France, a bizarre event occurred where a large group of people started uncontrollably dancing in the streets. It lasted for weeks, after which the people collapsed from exhaustion.

THE BURIAL OF THE SARDINE

In some Hispanic cultures, a humorous ritual known as the **Burial of the Sardine** (Entierro de la Sardina) takes place during the Carnival season.

ASHES IN PRINGLE CAN

Fredric Baur, the American food scientist and chemist who invented the iconic Pringles can in 1966, had an unusual final wish. He requested to have some of his ashes buried in one of his own Pringles cans - a wish which his family honoured after he died in 2008.

"NEVER GO TO A DOCTOR
WHOSE OFFICE PLANTS
HAVE DIED."

ERMA BOMBECK

BANANA PEEL ACCIDENTS

The comedic trope of slipping on a **banana peel** originates from real incidents in the early twentieth century when discarded banana peels caused accidents.

MOONING OF THE AMTRAK

In **Laguna Niguel**, California, a recurring event involved hundreds of people mooning passing Amtrak trains. This peculiar tradition lasted for over 30 years before being officially banned in 2010.

WEIGHING-IN CEREMONY
IN HIGH WYCOMBE

In this unique **English** tradition, the mayor is
publicly weighed annually to see if they've been
living a frugal life or indulging
at the taxpayers' expense.

THOMAS FITZPATRICK
LANDS PLANE ON NEW YORK STREET

In 1956, **Thomas Fitzpatrick**, in an inebriated state, made an audacious decision to steal a small plane. Flying it over New York City, he astoundingly landed it perfectly on the street in front of a bar, leaving his friends and bystanders in awe of his spontaneous and extraordinary aviation skills.

ANDREW JACKSON'S PARROT

At US President **Andrew Jackson's** funeral in 1845, his pet parrot had to be removed because it was swearing loudly.

TRAILERS

Movie trailers were originally shown after the movie. That's why they're called "trailers"!

"I LIKE LONG WALKS,
ESPECIALLY WHEN THEY
ARE TAKEN BY PEOPLE
WHO ANNOY ME."

FRED ALLEN

SHORTEST REIGN IN HISTORY

Louis XIX of France became king on 2 August 1830, after his father Charles X abdicated. He abdicated in favour of his nephew just 20 minutes later, making his reign the shortest of any monarch in history.

"AS YOU GET OLDER, THREE THINGS HAPPEN. THE FIRST IS YOUR MEMORY GOES, AND I CAN'T REMEMBER THE OTHER TWO."

SIR NORMAN WISDOM

SOLAR ECLIPSE WINS A WAR

During a battle in the six-year war between the **Medes** and the **Lydians** in 585 BC, a solar eclipse occurred, casting an unexpected darkness over the battlefield. Both sides interpreted the sudden darkness as a sign from the gods, signalling their disapproval of the war. The two sides ceased fighting immediately and negotiated a truce.

UNUSUAL SPORTS

Cheese Rolling: (England)

Wife Carrying: (Finland)

Octopush (Underwater Hockey): (England)

Kabaddi: (India)

Bog Snorkelling: (Wales)

LONELIEST TREE ON EARTH

The **Sitka spruce** on Campbell Island
(over 600 kilometres south of New Zealand) is
known as the loneliest tree on Earth.

LONGEST DRIVING BAN IN THE UK

The **longest driving ban** ever given to a
person in the UK is 80 years.

LARGE NOSE

In ancient **Rome**, a large nose was seen as a sign
of strength, power and leadership.
Take that, plastic surgeons!

EXAMPLES OF SARCASM

'If you find it hard to laugh at yourself, I would be happy to do it for you.' **(Groucho Marx)**

'History teaches us that men and nations behave wisely once they have exhausted all other alternatives.' **(Abba Eban)**

'I cannot speak well enough to be unintelligible.' **(Jane Austen, Northanger Abbey)**

'When one door closes, another opens. Or you can open the closed door. That's how doors work.' **(Unknown)**

ONE-HIT WONDERS

'**Video Killed the Radio Star**' by The Buggles

'**Mambo No. 5**' by Lou Bega

'**Macarena**' by Los del Río

'**Spirit In The Sky**' by Norman Greenbaum

'**The Hustle**' by Van McCoy

'**Who Let The Dogs Out**' by Baha Men

'**It's Raining Men**' by The Weather Girls

ODD WORLD RECORDS

The largest gathering of people
dressed as **penguins**.

Youngstown State University earned a Guinness
World Record, on 28 October 2017, for the
largest gathering of people dressed as penguins:
972 to be exact!

Longest continuous line of **hot dogs**.

A record was set with a continuous line of
hot dogs measuring 1,464.03 metres long.
This extraordinary feat resulted from a unique
collaboration, creating a tasty display that
spelled out "Hot Dog".

UNUSUAL SPORTING MASCOTS

The **'Fighting Pickles'** represent the University of North Carolina School of the Arts.

The **'Banana Slugs'** are the mascots of the University of California, Santa Cruz.

The '**Fighting Okra**' represents Delta State University in Cleveland, Mississippi.

I DON'T HAVE A
BUCKET LIST.

ONLY A 'DAM IT' LIST.

CROCODILE TONGUES

Unlike us, **crocodiles** can't stick out their tongues! Their tongues are firmly attached to the roof of their mouth, which keeps them neatly tucked in place, making any tongue-wagging antics utterly impossible.

UNORTHODOX RELIGION

Dudeism, a philosophy based on
'The Dude' from 'The Big Lebowski'.

ZOMBIES EAT BRAINS.

DON'T WORRY, MOST OF
YOU HAVE NOTHING TO
WORRY ABOUT.

KINGLY DEATHS

King Edmund II of England, believed to have been assassinated in 1016 while using the toilet.

King Adolf Frederick of Sweden, who reportedly ate himself to death.

BAT BOMB

An American **Second World War** project sought
to create a bomb filled with bats armed with
small incendiary devices, intended to be
released over Japanese cities.

"THE FUNDAMENTAL CAUSE OF THE TROUBLE IS THAT IN THE MODERN WORLD THE STUPID ARE COCKSURE WHILE THE INTELLIGENT ARE FULL OF DOUBT."

BERTRAND RUSSELL

ATTEMPTS TO SUE GOD

1. Ernie Chambers vs God (2007):
Nebraska State Senator Ernie Chambers filed a lawsuit against God in 2007, seeking a permanent injunction against God's harmful activities. The case was eventually dismissed, stating that God had no fixed address and could not be properly notified.

2. Pavel M. vs God (2005):
In Romania, a man named Pavel M., serving a sentence for murder, attempted to sue God for 'fraud, betrayal of trust, corruption, and influence peddling'. The case was dismissed because God is not a person or company and does not fall under the jurisdiction of the court.

WOJTEK, THE SOLDIER BEAR

During the Second World War, a unique member joined the Polish Army's 22nd Transport Company – he was an adopted bear named **Wojtek**. He carried heavy artillery shells, learned to salute, and participated in the Battle of Monte Cassino in Italy, contributing to the morale of the troops. Wojtek was officially enlisted as a private with his own paybook. Following the war, he spent his later years in Edinburgh Zoo in Scotland.

THE LONDON BEER FLOOD

An event of extraordinary circumstances occurred in **1814** when a huge brewery vat exploded, causing the streets of London to flood with beer. The massive wave of alcohol led to fatalities and substantial destruction in the area.

THE 'BICYCLE FACE' PANIC

As the **bicycle's** popularity soared in the late nineteenth century, so did societal fears, particularly those surrounding women cyclists. One peculiar anxiety was the so-called 'bicycle face' – a supposed medical condition. Doctors of the era warned that the strain and concentration needed for women to ride bicycles could lead to a permanently anxious and unattractive expression, characterised by clenched jaws and bulging eyes.

"In life, on some days
you will be the pigeon
and on other days you
will be the statue."

Anonymous

I AM NOT LAZY.

I AM USING
ENERGY-SAVING MODE.

BATTLE OF KARÁNSEBES

In 1788, in a rather unusual turn of events,
Austrian troops became embroiled in a friendly
fire incident over a dispute regarding alcohol.
This confusion led to significant
self-inflicted injuries.

CHICKEN GUN

The **Chicken Gun**, a device used in aviation safety testing, shoots frozen chickens at aircraft windshields and engines using a compressed air cannon to test structural integrity and safety under bird-strike scenarios.

BOATY MCBOATFACE

In a 2016 online poll by the Natural Environment Research Council, the name '**Boaty McBoatface**' emerged victorious for the naming of a polar research vessel. The new ship was eventually named 'RRS Sir David Attenborough'.

URINE TAX

The **Romans** used urine for many things, including tanning leather and washing clothes. This is due to the ammonia that urine contains. Urine was so important that Emperor Nero even introduced a tax on the collection and disposal of urine.

"BOTH OPTIMISTS AND PESSIMISTS CONTRIBUTE TO OUR SOCIETY. THE OPTIMIST INVENTS THE AEROPLANE AND THE PESSIMIST THE PARACHUTE."

GEORGE BERNARD SHAW